The
Lance

CHRISTIAN SPIRITUALITY SERIES

Brother Ramon SSF

> Praying the Jesus Prayer
> Remember Me
> Life's Changing Seasons
> Praying the Bible

Tony Castle

> Evelyn Underhill on Prayer
> Thomas Merton on Prayer
> The Prayers of Christina Rossetti

The Prayers of Lancelot Andrewes

Compiled and edited

by

Tony Castle

Marshall Pickering

Marshall Morgan and Scott
Marshall Pickering
32–42 Cleveland Street
London W1P 5FB

Copyright © 1989 Tony Castle

First published in 1989 by Marshall Morgan and Scott Publications Ltd
Part of the Marshall Pickering Holdings Group

All rights reserved. No part of this publication may be reproduced, stored in a retrieval system, or transmitted, in any form or by any means, electronic, mechanical, photocopying, recording or otherwise, without the prior permission in writing, of the publisher

British Library CIP Data
Andrewes, Lancelot, *1555–1626*
  The prayers of Lancelot Andrewes
  1. Christian life. Prayers – Devotional works
  I. Title II. Castle, Tony, *1938–*
  III. Series
  242'.8

ISBN: 0-551-01765-1

Text Set in Baskerville by Avocet Robinson
Printed in Great Britain by Henry Ling Ltd, at the Dorset Press, Dorchester, Dorset.

Contents

Introduction	7
Lancelot Andrewes: Man of Prayer	9
The Prayers of Lancelot Andrewes	
Thoughts on Prayer	13
Thank You	13
Faith	14
Faith	15
Hope	16
Hope	16
Love of God	17
Sorrow for Sin	17
The Dial	18
Adoration of the Holy Trinity	20
Praise	21
Praise	22
Morning Prayer	23
On Waking	23
Lines of Meditation on Prayer	24
Meditation on the Lord's Prayer	25
Grace before a Meal	26
For Unity	27
An Appeal for Help	27
Commendation	27
Scripture Sources	29

Introduction

Bishop Andrewes compiled his prayers for his own personal use. Were he among us today, nearly four hundred years after he started writing them, he would be amazed to see this neat little collection introducing him and his prayers to the modern Christian.

While Lancelot Andrewes' erudition and deep knowledge of the Bible was impressive, it is the memory of his sanctity, achieved by systematically setting time aside for prayer, which lives on in the Church. Were he guiding a diocese today as a pastoral bishop I am certain that he would be in the forefront of the work for Christian Unity. In his own lifetime he battled intellectually with Roman Catholic theologians, but would today draw great joy from the wonderful co-operation in Biblical Studies and the daily witness of Christians of all traditions praying together.

I hope that he would also be happy to know that it is a Roman Catholic editor that wanted to make a selection of his Bible-based prayers available to all Christians of whatever tradition.

Bishop Andrewes often gave the Biblical source of his prayers alongside the prayer; for convenience these are gathered on a separate page at the back.

I would like to thank Jacquie Galley for typing the manuscript for me.

Lancelot Andrewes: Man of Prayer

The *Preces Privatae* (Private Prayers) of Lancelot Andrewes were never intended for publication. They were written and used each day by Lancelot Andrewes during the five hours he daily spent in prayer. After his death his friends commented that this compilation of his private prayers was seldom from his hand; at his funeral John Buckeridge, Bishop of Ely, said 'Lancelot's life was a life of prayer.'

Selections from *Preces Privatae* were first published in the original Greek, Latin and Hebrew in which they were written, in 1668, (forty-two years after the author's death). The first complete publication of the original text in English appeared in 1899. The Prayers were adapted for the modern reader in F. E. Brightman's English edition of 1903. This present small selection, again adapted for today's reader, is taken from the 1903 publication.

Lancelot Andrewes was born in 1555 at Thames Street, Barking, and went to school, first at the Coopers' Free School, Stepney and then he progressed to the Merchant Taylors' School. At sixteen years of age he went to Cambridge on a scholarship, later the same year, 1571, he was nominated by the Queen, Elizabeth I, to a scholarship at Jesus College, Oxford. There he took his degree, four years later, and was elected a Fellow of Pembroke Hall. He studied and taught there for the next ten years, developing into one of the English Church's foremost theologians and preachers.

On holiday in East London in 1580 he experienced the earthquake of that year and witnessed the destruction of part of St Paul's cathedral. This made a great impression upon him and sometime in the next five years he was ordained for the Anglican

Ministry. Not long after ordination he became chaplain to Whitgift, the Archbishop of Canterbury and then the Queen. His connections at court led to his appointment to St Giles, Cripplegate, London and he served other benefices. What gave Lancelot particular pleasure, as a scholar and a university man, was his election to the post of Master of his College in 1589. (A post he held for sixteen years.)

In 1604 Lancelot was appointed one of the translators of what became known as the Authorised, or King James, version of the Bible, published in 1611. At this time, on behalf of King James I, whom he impressed with his learning and obvious piety, he became the Nation's foremost controversialist. The eminent Roman Catholic scholar Cardinal Robert Bellarmine had corresponded with the King, and James handed the theological debate over to Bishop Andrewes, as he had become in 1609. On behalf of the Church of England he conducted a long and exhaustive debate with Bellarmine.

Consecrated first to the See of Chichester, he was translated to Ely, and eventually, 1618, to Winchester. Had he not been so outspoken about the lack of learning and the worldly life of the episcopate in general, and resisted all political efforts to manipulate him and co-operate with the Crown in reducing the authority of the Church, he would have risen to the highest ecclesiastical appointment in the Country.

Although a great scholar and the most influential preacher of his time he will always be best remembered for his personal sanctity. He died on 26th September 1626, and was buried in St Saviour's Church, Southwark, London.

Three aspects of Bishop Andrewes life are usually commented on: his scholarship; his pastoral role as bishop; and his outstanding sanctity of life.

Fluent in Greek, Latin and Hebrew (in which his *Preces* was written) he also had a grasp of most European languages. His published sermons, works of theology and prayers reveal a man with an incredible detailed knowledge of the Bible. While he criticised the teaching of the Puritans, most of his theological work was aimed at answering Roman Catholic doctrine and apologetics.

As a Churchman Andrewes was the most outstanding of his age. A man of great integrity he did much by exhortation and example to raise the poor standard of clerical life. He was popularly known for his long detailed sermons, over which he took great pains, which were another extension of his life of prayer.

The zeal and piety of 'Good Bishop' Andrewes was recognised and won the respect of his contempories. His spiritual life was totally grounded in a deep knowledge and love of Holy Scripture. Without doubt Lancelot Andrewes was one of the finest scholars and most saintly pastoral bishops the Anglican Church has ever produced.

The full text of *Preces* was written in Greek, with some Latin and Hebrew. Bishop Andrewes appears to have prayed in Greek and he often defended the original languages of the Bible against the extreme Protestants of the time who condemned the use of Latin and Greek.

Little of the *Preces* is original. The prayers are a mosaic of quotations mostly, but not entirely, from the Bible. They are incredibly constructed from thousands of Biblical quotations with occasional material from Collections of Prayers from the Orthodox and the Roman Catholic Church.

The full text of Lancelot Andrewes prayers would not, as they were originally written, appeal to the modern Christian. It is hoped however, that this small selection will be useful to many readers.

Thoughts on Prayer

Samuel was among those who called on his name. (Ps 99:6)

As for me, far be it from me that
I should sin against the Lord
by ceasing to pray for you. (1 Sam 12:23)

We will devote ourselves to prayer
and to the ministry of the word. (Acts 6:4)

Thou who hearest prayer,
   to thee shall all flesh come.
When our sins prevail over us,
   thou doest forgive them. (Ps 65:2)

O Lord, open my lips
and my mouth shall show forth thy praise. (Ps 51:15)

Thank You

I thank you for the sayings:

> For God sent the Son into the world, not to condemn the world, but that the world might be saved through him.

> I did not come to judge the world, but to save the world.

> I came not to call the righteous, but sinners.

> The Son of man came to seek and to save the lost.

Come to me, all who labour and are heavy burdened,
>   and I will give you rest.

>   He who comes to me I will not cast out.

>   Father, forgive them, for they know not what they do.

>   Today you will be with me in Paradise.

>   I choose to give to the last as I give to you.

Faith

I believe,
>   with David, that I shall see the goodness
>   >   of the Lord in the land of the living.
>   with Paul, that Christ Jesus came into the
>   >   world to save sinners.
>   with John, that if any one sins we have
>   >   an advocate with the Father, Jesus Christ;
>   >   and he is the expiation for our sins and
>   >   for the whole world.
>   with Peter that you are the Christ,
>   >   the Son of the living God.
>   with Nathaniel, that you are the Son of God,
>   >   the King of Israel.
>   with the Samaritans, that this is indeed the Christ,
>   >   the Saviour of the world.
>   with Matthew, that you are the Christ, the Son of God
>   >   who is coming into the world.
>   with the Apostles and Elders, that we shall be saved
>   >   through the grace of the Lord Jesus.
>   with Andrew, that I have found the Christ.

We have believed in Christ Jesus, to be justified by faith in Christ and not by works of the law.

We believe that there is one God and one mediator between God and men, Christ Jesus, who gave Himself as a ransom for all.

We believe that faith is active along with works and by works is made perfect.

Faith

I believe that you created me;
I am the work of your hands,
   do not neglect me.

I believe that I am made
in your image and likeness;
   do not wipe out that image within me.

I believe that you redeemed me
at the price of your blood;
   do not pay such a price in vain.

I believe that as a Christian
I bear your name
   do not permit me to do anything to dishonour it.

I believe that I am a branch of the tree
of the Christian family
   do not allow me to be cut off from you.

Hope

In you, Lord, I seek refuge, let me never
   be put to shame.
You have been my hope since I was at
   my mother's breast.
So, Lord, remember your word to me in which
   I have always trusted.
You have said, there is hope for my future;
because your love has been poured out,
giving us grounds for hope and in this hope
   we are saved.
The Lord of hope will fill me with
   joy and peace.
Even if I am beset with difficulties
   I will trust.
You are always the Saviour of those
   who seek you,
Who wait upon you as their help and shield.
No evil will come upon me because
   the Lord is my refuge,
My trust is in Him at all times.

Hope

Our forefathers hoped in you,
they trusted you and you helped them.
They called out to you and their hope was fulfilled.
We hope in you as they did, may this trust keep us safe.

Love of God

You, my God, I love for your own sake and above everything. It is you that I desire as the end purpose of my life. Always and in all things I seek to find you and your love; with my whole heart and soul and with unbroken effort.

What will you provide as the meaning and purpose of my life? If you do not give Yourself to me, you give nothing; if I find anything but You, I find nothing. No other reward will do. The hope of finding and possessing You has kept me going. Now, if you deny me Yourself, after entertaining so high a hope, I am left with nothing.

Shall I find life empty, void and meaningless? Emptiness and sadness do not belong to You; they are not signs of Your presence.

Make me, O most loving God, here and now, love You, before and above all things. Make me to seek You in everything and everyone; and, at the end of my life to possess You who are Love, forever.

Sorrow for Sin

I have sinned, Lord, I have sinned against You
   and You have not punished me as I deserve.
   I am ashamed of my sin
   and I will turn away
   and return to find you again.
To you I return saying,
   I have done what is wrong
   I have behaved badly
   and now I seek you
   with all my heart and with all my strength.

From your holy dwelling place, hear my prayer, O Lord,
> hear the pleading of your servant
> and heal me,

I do not presume to lift my eyes to the heavens,
> but stand with the publican, beat my breast
> and say, 'God, be merciful to me a sinner'.

The Dial

You who hold all times, all earth's seasons, in the
> palm of your hand;
> > give us time and opportunity for prayer,
> > > and save us.

You who were born at dead of night,
> give us the grace to be born anew
> each day by the power of the Holy Spirit
> so that Christ may be formed in us,
> > and save us.

You who rose from the dead very early in the morning
> while the sun was still rising;
> help us to die to ourselves and rise
> up each day to newness of life,
> > and save us.

You who, at the third hour of the day, sent
> down the Holy Spirit upon the Apostles,
> do not take that same Spirit from us,
> but renew it within us every day,
> > and save us.

You who, at the sixth hour on the sixth day,
 allowed yourself to be nailed, with our sins
 to the cross;
 take all our sins away,
  and save us.

You who, at the ninth hour, tasted death
 for us sinners and our sins;
 help us to die to sin and everything
 which is contrary to your will,
  and save us.

You who, early in the evening, willed to be
 taken down from the cross and buried;
 take away our sins and bury them
 in your tomb,
  and save us.

You who, at supper time, instituted the most sacred
 mysteries of your body and blood;
 help us to keep the memory and be sharers
 in those same mysteries, never to our own
 judgement but for the remission of our sins,
  and save us.

You who, late in the night, breathed upon your Apostles
 and conferred the authority to forgive
 and retain sins;
 help us, sharing in that authority, to remit
 sin and retain none,
  and save us.

You who promised that the Bridegroom will come at midnight;
 grant that the cry, 'Here's the Bridegroom!
 Come out to meet him!' will echo in our ears
 and find us prepared to meet Him,
  and save us.

You who have foretold that you will come for judgement on a
   day and at an hour that we least expect;
   make us prepared every day and every hour
   to be ready for your coming,
      and save us.

Adoration of the Holy Trinity

O God the Father,
   who has wonderfully created out of nothing,
   who governs and maintains the Universe with your power,
   who surrendered your Son to death for us,
   – your majesty is unspeakable,
   – your power is incomparable,
   – your goodness is immeasurable.

O God the Son,
   who was born of the virgin,
   who has washed us in your precious blood,
   who conquered death by your victorious
      rising and ascension,
   – your majesty is unspeakable,
   – your power is incomparable,
   – your goodness is immeasurable.

O God the Holy Spirit,
   who descended upon Jesus as a dove,
   who appeared above the Apostles as tongues of fire,
   who visits and strengthens the hearts of believers,
   – your majesty is unspeakable,
   – your power is incomparable,
   – your goodness is immeasurable.

O Blessed Trinity, Father so good,
              Son so loving,
              Spirit so kind,
  your work is life
  your love is grace
  your contemplation is glory.
  You I worship.
  You I acknowledge with all the love of my heart.

Praise

I praise you Almighty God for your Divine Attributes,

– for your Majesty:
    Father, glorify thou me in thy own
    presence with the glory which I had with
    thee before the world was made.

– for your eternity:
    Call on the name of the Lord, the everlasting
    God.

– for your presence everywhere:
    Do I not fill heaven and earth?

– for your knowledge of all:
    Lord, you know everything.

– for your mighty power:
    With God nothing is impossible.

– for your wisdom:
    O the depth of the riches and
    wisdom, and knowledge of God!
    How unsearchable are his judgements
    and how inscrutable his ways!

– for your truth:
  Heaven and earth will pass away,
  but my words will not pass away.

– for your infinite love:
  His steadfast love endures forever.

– for your righteousness:
  His righteousness endures for ever.

– for your mercy:
  Be merciful, even as your Father is merciful.
  Who is like thee, O Lord,

  Who is like thee, majestic in holiness,
  terrible in glorious deeds, doing wonders.

Praise

Blessed art thou, O lord,
the God of Israel, our Father,
  for ever and ever.

There, O Lord, is the greatness
  and the might
  and the glory
  and the victory
  and the majesty
and the praise and the strength
for all that is in heaven and earth is thine.
Thine is the kingdom, O Lord, and Thou art above all.

Morning Prayer

You, Lord, who hear prayer,
  to you all mankind must come.
I will pray in the morning and evening
  and you will hear my prayer:
to you I will offer a sacrifice,
  let my prayer rise up like incense before you,
because you have been my helper.
  I have thought upon your goodness
and I will pray in the morning and evening.

I thank you, Almightly Lord, everlasting God,
  for you have kept me safe throughout the night;
not because of any merits of mine,
  but out of your own mercy and love.
Grant, Lord, that I may so pass this day
  serving you, that my faithfulness to my duties
and obedience to you may please you.

On Waking

O Lord, send forth your light, create the morning
  and make the sun to rise on the good
  and the bad; enlighten the blindness of our minds
  with the knowledge of your truth.
  Let the light of your face shine upon us
  for in your light we see light,
  so that one day we may live in the light of your
  grace and glory.

Lines of Meditation on Prayer

You are concerned about so much, but only one thing is
   necessary
That we give ourselves continually to prayer and to the
ministry
   of the word.
Therefore, watch and pray always, so that you may
be counted worthy to escape what is to come.

Love the Lord, devote your life to Him and lean upon Him
   for your salvation.
Be humble, all you have has been given to you.
If the sinless Christ prayed how much more ought I,
   a sinner, pray.
But be encouraged, God is a hearer,
   not of the voice but of the heart.
More is achieved by the direction of the heart
   than by words.
In this Christ set us the example.

Our bodily posture does nothing for God; the
   profit from that is ours.
Prayer ascends, God's mercy descends.
God's generosity is more abundant than our prayer;
He always gives more than he is asked for.

God wants us to ask and teaches us what to ask for and
promises that He will hear us. We know this and yet
we do not ask.

Prayer is a summary of faith and an expression of Hope.
Faith is expressed in prayer and grounded in prayer, therefore,
work at prayer, remembering the words, 'always pray and not
   give up'.
Faith is the foundation of prayer and the foundation of
Faith is the promise of God.
Lift up your Hearts.
He who made us, taught us to pray.
The prayer of the humble pierces the clouds
and develops the relationship with God.

Meditation on the Lord's Prayer

Our Father:
    You are holy. Your name is above every name,
    to be held in veneration and awe.
    But I have not accorded it such honour
    and now I whole-heartedly confess
    and humbly promise to make your name
    the centre of all that I do, so that
    your name may be hallowed.

Thy Kingdom:
    It is the object of my desires, to come
    to share, one day, in your glory; may it come
    now to me as a share in your grace.
    May this same grace help me here and now,
    to live in such a way that I may attain
    a place in heaven, even among the least of the saints.

Thy Will:
    May your holy gracious will be done by all upon earth.
    Let my own will depart from me.

Give us and forgive us:
> May your heavenly food sustain us;
> give us all that is necessary for health and peace.
> Forgive me the huge debts of the past, the
> shameful falls, the frequent lapses.
> If you, Lord, keep a record of our sins
> > who will survive,
> but with the Lord there is mercy and the
> > fullness of salvation.

Lead us not:
> Never permit me, Lord, so aware of my
> pitiful weakness, to fall into temptation.

Deliver us from evil:
> Deliver me from all evil
> - the evil within myself
> - the evil from the devil's temptations
> - the evil of worldliness
> - the evil of disease.
>
> Evils, past, present and to come,
> > from them all, Lord deliver me.

Grace before a Meal

Lord, you give food to all of the living
> and feed the young ravens that call upon You,
> as we called upon you in our youth;
> fulfil our needs and grant
> that our hearts may be filled
> with the joy of your presence.

For Unity

Give light to those whose eyes are darkened
    and live in the shadow of death.
Guide our feet in the way of peace
    that we may seek what unites us.
If there be disagreement let us seek
    to maintain order and decency
and all that edifies and gives glory to God.

An Appeal for Help

O God, you know how foolish I can be
and my sins are not hidden from you.
Lord, you can read my heart and my secret
longings and private complaints are known to you.
May no one who hopes and trusts in you
be caused any harm because of me.
On my part I offer my prayer trusting
in your steadfast love for an answer.
Save me from sinking further into the mire
and from being overwhelmed by the problems
and difficulties that fill my life.
Do not hide your face from me but draw
near and set me free.
O Lord, make haste to help me.

Commendation

Lord, I commend into your care and keeping,
- my soul and body, may all my impulses be yours.
- my mind and thoughts, may all my opportunities
    for prayer be yours.

- my promises and prayers, may all my intentions be yours.
- my limbs and senses, may all I attempt be yours.
- my comings and goings, may all my words and actions be yours.
- my life and death, may all my pastime actions be yours.
- my brothers and sisters and their families.
- my friends, neighbours, well-wishers and all God's people,
  may we all be yours.

Scripture Sources

Provided by Lancelot Andrewes alongside many of the prayers

Thank you

Jn 3:17/Jn 12:47/Mt 9:13/Lk 19:10/Mt 11:28/Jn 6:37/
Lk 23:34/Lk 23:43/Mt 20:14

Faith

Ps 27:13/1 Tim 1:15/1 Jn 2:2/Mt 16:16/Jn 1:49/Jn 4:42/
Jn 11:27/Acts 15:11/Jn 1:41/Gal 2:16/1 Tim 2:5/
James 2:22

Hope

Ps 31:1/Ps 22:9/Ps 119:49/Jer 31:17/Rom 5:5/Rom 15:13/
Job 13:15/Ps 17:7/Ps 33:20/Ps 91:9/Ps 62:8

An Act of Sorrow for Sin

Ps 41:4/Bar 2:30/2 Chron 6:38/2 Chron 7:14/Lk 18:13.

Praise

Jn 17:5/Gen 14:18/Jer 23:24/Jn 21:17/Lk 1:37/Rom 11:33/
Mt 24:35/Ps 118:1/Ps 111:3/Lk 6:36/Ex 15:11

Praise (II)

1 Chron 29:10

The Dial

Acts 1:7/Ps 32:7/Tit 3:5/Gal 4:19/Eph 4:13/Mk 16:2/
Rom 6:4/Col 2:14/Acts 10:11/Gal 2:15/Jn 4:52/
Col 3:5/Acts 3:1/Jn 1:39/Jn 19:38/Jn 13:2/Jn 20:19/
Mt 25:6/Lk 12:46

Morning Prayer

Ps 65:2/Ps 5:3/Ps 141:2/Ps 63:6

Thoughts on Prayer

Ps 99:6/1 Sam 12:23/Acts 6:4/Ps 65:2/Ps 51:15

An Appeal for Help

Ps 69:5/Ps 38:9/Ps 69:6/Ps 69:13/Ps 69:18